History

FOR COMMON ENTRANCE

13+

Exam Practice Questions

Gavin Hannah

GALORE PARK

AN HACHETTE UK COMPANY

The publishers would like to thank the following for permission to reproduce copyright material:

Photo credits p3 © The Gallery Collection/Corbis **p5** © Bridgeman Art Library, London / SuperStock **p7** Richard the Lionheart (1157-99) during the First Crusade (gouache on paper), Jackson, Peter (1922-2003) / Private Collection / © Look and Learn / The Bridgeman Art Library **p9** MS. 6, fol.136v Murder of St Thomas a Becket, from the St Alban's Chronicle (vellum), English School, (15th century) / © Lambeth Palace Library, London, UK / The Bridgeman Art Library **p11** © Universal Images Group/Getty Images **p13** The Black Death, English School, (20th century) / Private Collection / © Look and Learn / The Bridgeman Art Library **p15** Ms 6 f.243 Battle of Agincourt, 1415, English with Flemish illuminations, from the 'St. Alban's Chronicle' (vellum), English School, (15th century) / © Lambeth Palace Library, London, UK / The Bridgeman Art Library **p17** © British Library/Robana/Hulton Fine Art Collection/Getty Images **p19** © The Bridgeman Art Library/Getty Images **p23** © National Archives **p25** © DEA / G. DAGLI ORTI/Getty Images **p27** Spoilation of a shrine, illustration from 'The Church of England: A History for the People' by H.D.M. Spence-Jones, pub. c.1910 (litho) (sepia photo), English School, (20th century) / Private Collection / © The Stapleton Collection / The Bridgeman Art Library **p29** © Culture Club/Hulton Archive/Getty Images **p31** © Heritage Image Partnership Ltd / Alamy **p33** © Hulton Archive/Getty Images **p35** Execution of Strafford, May 12 1641 (engraving) (b/w photo), Hollar, Wenceslaus (1607-77) / Private Collection / © The Bridgeman Art Library **p37** Execution of king Charles I at Whitehall (engraving), English School, (18th century) / Private Collection / © Look and Learn / Peter Jackson Collection / The Bridgeman Art Library **p39** The Great Plague: Scenes in the Streets of London (engraving), English School, (19th century) / Private Collection / © Look and Learn / The Bridgeman Art Library **p41** © Lieve Verschuier/The Bridgeman Art Library/Getty Images **p43** © John Wootton/The Bridgeman Art Library/Getty Images **p45** © Mary Evans Picture Library / Alamy **p49** © Anonymous/The Bridgeman Art Library/Getty Images **p51** © Punch / TopFoto **p53** © The Granger Collection, NYC / TopFoto **p55** Thomas Duncombe (1796-1861) Presenting the Chartists' Petition on 2nd May 1842 (engraving) (b/w photo), English School, (19th century) / © Museum of London, UK / The Bridgeman Art Library **p57** © The Art Gallery Collection / Alamy **p59** © Universal History Archive/Getty Images **p61** © MPI/Archive Photos/Getty Images **p63** The Fleet Sewer, c.1840 (w/c on paper), English School, (19th century) / © London Metropolitan Archives, City of London / The Bridgeman Art Library **p65** Glass-Smashing for Votes! Suffragettes as Window-Breakers, 1912 (litho), Lunt, Wilmot (fl.1900-17) (after) / © The Illustrated London News Picture Library, London, UK / The Bridgeman Art Library

Acknowledgements p6 John Cannon (editor): from *The Oxford Companion to British History* (Oxford University Press, 1997); **p10** Michael Lumb: from *All Our Yesterdays: Introducing English History* (Hallmark Press, 2008); **p12** Roy Strong: from *The Story of Britain: A People's History* (Hutchinson, in association with Julia MacRae, 1996), reproduced by permission of Penguin Random House; **p36** L. E. Snellgrove: from *The Early Modern Age*, 2nd Revised Edition (Longman, 1992), reproduced by permission of the publisher; **p56** H.L. Peacock: from *History of Modern Britain 1815–1975*, 3rd Edition (Heinemann, 1976).

Every effort has been made to trace all copyright holders, but if any have been inadvertently overlooked the publishers will be pleased to make the necessary arrangements at the first opportunity.

Although every effort has been made to ensure that website addresses are correct at time of going to press, Galore Park cannot be held responsible for the content of any website mentioned in this book. It is sometimes possible to find a relocated web page by typing in the address of the home page for a website in the URL window of your browser.

Hachette UK's policy is to use papers that are natural, renewable and recyclable products and made from wood grown in sustainable forests. The logging and manufacturing processes are expected to conform to the environmental regulations of the country of origin.

Orders: please contact Bookpoint Ltd, 130 Milton Park, Abingdon, Oxon OX14 4SB. Telephone: +44 (0)1235 827827. Lines are open 9.00a.m.–5.00p.m., Monday to Saturday, with a 24-hour message answering service. Visit our website at www.galorepark.co.uk for details of other revision guides for Common Entrance, examination papers and Galore Park publications.

Published by Galore Park Publishing Ltd
An Hachette UK company
Carmelite House, 50 Victoria Embankment, London, EC4Y 0DZ
www.galorepark.co.uk

Design and typography by DC Graphic Design Limited, Swanley Village, Kent

A catalogue record for this title is available from the British Library.

Printed and bound by CPI Group (UK) Ltd, Croydon, CR0 4YY

ISBN: 978 1 471809 05 7

About the author

Educated at the University of Birmingham, St. John's College, Cambridge and Kellogg College, Oxford, Gavin Hannah taught history in an IAPS school for 30 years. He has also worked in independent senior schools, examined history at A Level and trained as an ISI Inspector. In 1988, he was elected a Fellow of the Society of Antiquaries. He lives in Oxford.

Acknowledgements

Many people helped produce this book. In particular, my thanks go to the following: at Galore Park; Tammy Poggo, my editor, for her enthusiasm in driving the project forward; to Chris Scrace, for speedy responses to my suggestions; to Lesley Staff for unravelling textual and source queries. Bob Pace, of Belmont, Mill Hill Preparatory School, offered wise suggestions regarding the evidence questions. Nial Murphy, of Radley College, contributed some excellent final points. My pupils at Summer Fields endured much of the advice given in the introduction. Indeed, its final shape reflects their youthful experience and criticism. Finally, I thank my wife, Ann, for her tolerance and understanding while *History for Common Entrance 13+ Exam Practice Questions* dominated the household.

Gavin Hannah
Oxford
January 2014

For Jackson, Milo and Orlando

Contents

Introduction

This book is addressed primarily to the pupils who will be sitting the Common Entrance examination in history. However, teachers, tutors, parents, or indeed anyone else involved in preparation for the exam, will also find it useful.

The main aims of this book are as follows:

● to set out the structure and content of the new syllabus for Common Entrance history, effective from September 2013

● to outline some of the skills you will require when answering evidence questions

● to offer a suggested method of tackling evidence questions, in terms of how to structure and approach an answer

● to give you a selection of evidence questions in the new style. All the set Common Entrance evidence topics are covered. However, a wider selection is also offered in order to allow you to become familiar with their form and to practise and develop your answering skills

● to present some of the skills you will need when answering essay questions in the exam

● to provide you with a selection of new-style essay titles for further practice

The new syllabus

The revised syllabus, based on Key Stage 3 of the National Curriculum, came into force in September 2013. The first examination paper was set in autumn 2013 and the first major examination will be in the summer of 2014.

The complete syllabus may be found on the ISEB website: www.iseb.co.uk

The syllabus covers English and British History during the period 1066–1914 and is divided into three named time periods:

● Medieval Realms: Britain 1066–1485

● The Making of the United Kingdom: 1485–1750

● Britain and Empire: 1750–1914

In each of the three time periods, there are five common study themes:

● war and rebellion

● government and parliament

● religion

● social history (social and economic history for the period 1750–1914)

● general topics, including local history

The new exam format

The examination paper will be 60 minutes long.
You must attempt:

● **ONE** evidence question

● **ONE** essay question.

It is suggested that you spend **5 minutes** reading and planning, then **20** minutes on the evidence question and **35** minutes on the essay question.

The evidence question (20 marks/20 minutes)

The evidence question will consist of two written sources (which may be contemporary, modern or a mix of both), and a third source that is pictorial. The question will always begin with the words: *'Using ALL the sources and your own knowledge ...'* and will ask you to consider a viewpoint derived from the sources.

In this exercise you will be expected to demonstrate the following skills:

● comprehension

● comparison and corroboration by cross-referencing sources

● differentiation between first-hand evidence and hindsight

● deduction and interpretation

● an understanding of provenance

● evaluation of the utility of the sources

● the ability to present an overview, supported by your own knowledge, which serves to place the sources into their historical context

When evaluating pieces of evidence with a specific question in mind, there are **four** main skills which you should note and seek to develop. These are: **comprehension**, **comparison**, the idea of the **utility** of a source in a given context, and the appropriate use of your **own knowledge**.

Comprehension means **understanding** the material. Without understanding, you cannot offer any meaningful responses. Regular practice with the appropriate sources will develop skills and techniques in this area. **Specialised vocabulary** for any particular period or topic should also be noted. For example, if you are learning about Thomas Becket, you should be familiar with the word 'martyr'. Likewise, when studying slavery you ought to know the meaning of the term 'Triangular Trade'.

Comparison means picking a clear theme or idea to compare. Remember that only two sources may be compared at any one time. You should get into the habit of cross-referencing sources with regard to one particular idea. You must consider the **differences** as well as the **similarities**. If you draw a rough table with rows and columns on a planning sheet, this will stop you trying to hold too many ideas in your head at the same time! Above all, be crystal clear about what it is you are trying to compare, otherwise your answer will be muddled.

Utility means **usefulness**. In evidence questions, it means how useful a particular source is **for a particular purpose**. You should always bear in mind the question which the examiners have set and assess the utility of the sources in relation to this. The **content** and **provenance** of a source are vital things to consider when judging the utility of a piece of evidence. If a source has good provenance, the chances are that it will be reliable. But be careful – reliability and usefulness are not the same thing. Even if reliable, a source may not necessarily be useful. It can only be useful if it is reliable **and** relevant to the particular question you are handling.

Your own knowledge will enable you to put the sources into their historical context, and as such is an important element when answering the evidence question. Each school year, the examination board sets two evidence question topics for each of the three historical eras. So you will be able to prepare the background history to your set topic.

All these skills can form part of a top-level answer if used properly. You should try to answer the question by making a judgement based on the direct use of the sources. Include valid statements on the reliability of the material, as well as relevant reference to your own background knowledge. Answers should be well structured with a clear beginning, middle and end.

The essay question (30 marks/35 minutes)

There will be ten essay titles from which you must select just **one**. Each question will be generic and open-ended. Up to 50 per cent of the marks could be awarded for good narrative. However, to produce a top-grade answer you should try to express opinions, formulate judgements and use your analytical skills to justify what you say.

Choose your essay question with care. Ensure that you are able to make a good and relevant essay from the title you choose and that you can relate your choice exactly to the question. For example, if you decide to write about the significance of the **consequences** of a war, make sure that the war you choose has plenty of consequences. Then, focus on them and their significance. Do not just tell the story of the war itself! Always ensure that you have enough material to write about. Can you say enough to answer the question thoroughly? Can it be relevant to the question?

Managing your time is important. Practise writing against the clock, particularly in the final run-up to the exams, and see how much you can write in a given amount of time. Having some idea of this will increase your confidence. If you qualify for extra time, make sure you follow the advice you are given on how to make the best use of it.

Make a **plan** to get a good structure. Include an **introduction** and a **conclusion** with reference to the essay title. Between these there should be a series of **linked paragraphs**, each making a particular point and following on from the last in a logical way to form a clear framework of argument.

Narrative is important, indeed it is possible to score 50 per cent of the marks allowed for the essay for good narrative alone. But story telling on its own does not make a top-grade answer, so avoid this. Ensure that historical material is carefully used to underpin your arguments and to support your opinions. Comment on what you write and try to understand its importance in relation to the question. Do not make generalisations, and always have a piece of evidence to support what you say.

Be relevant, and use precisely selected knowledge. Keep a sense of focus. Produce a **question-led response**. Appreciate the difference between **Topic knowledge** and **Question knowledge**. Topic knowledge means everything you have been taught about a topic, such as Medieval monasteries or Robert Walpole and his policies. Question knowledge means only the knowledge necessary to answer a particular question on that topic.

Above everything else, enjoy what you write and let that sparkle come through your script. After all, you have chosen to tackle that particular essay. Good luck!

EVIDENCE QUESTIONS
MEDIEVAL REALMS: BRITAIN
1066–1485

1 The Norman Conquest

Read the introduction and the sources and then answer the question which follows.

→ ## Introduction

On Saturday, 14 October 1066, Duke William of Normandy and his army won a decisive victory over the Anglo-Saxon forces led by King Harold. Throughout the day, the English army with their impressive shield wall defended the ridge at Senlac Hill. Finally, overwhelmed by superior military discipline and the skills of the Norman archers and cavalry, the English forces were annihilated and Harold was killed.

Source A: an extract from William of Poitiers, a Norman priest who became a chaplain to William the Conqueror. He was not present at the Battle of Hastings. He wrote his account around 1071 and his story is inspired by his admiration for Duke William.

Evening was now falling and the English saw they could not hold out much longer against the Normans. They knew they had lost a great part of their army, and also that their king with his two brothers and many of their greatest men had fallen. Dismayed at the heroic courage of the duke, who spared none who came against him, they began to fly as swiftly as they could, some on horseback and some on foot. Many lay on the ground bathed in blood. Many left their corpses in the depths of the forest. Many, fallen on the ground, were trampled to death under the hooves of horses. The brave Normans carried on their pursuit, striking the English rebels in the back and bringing a happy end to this famous victory.

Source B: an extract from a modern historian writing about the achievements of the Normans after the Battle of Hastings.

King William's first task was to reward the Norman and French barons who had fought with him. He gave them lands taken from English thanes [Saxon lords] who had died in battle. William's barons were hated foreigners so they built castles and shut themselves away whenever danger threatened. William's barons were not given land for nothing. William made more definite arrangements and they had to provide a certain number of mounted knights to raise an army for their king. The need to give military service in return for land is known as the feudal system. William's clerks made a great survey which came to be known as the Domesday Book. A new language, Norman French, was brought to England. Under bishops and abbots from the Continent, the organisation of the English Church developed.

Source C: a nineteenth-century painting showing William the Conqueror leading his Norman knights against the English at Hastings during the Norman Conquest. Victory at this battle was total. The battleground was stained with the blood of the best of the English nobility.

Question

Using **ALL** the sources and your own knowledge, how true is it to say that the Battle of Hastings completed the Norman Conquest of England?

2 The First Crusade, 1095–99

Read the introduction and the sources and then answer the question which follows.

→ ## Introduction

In 1095, at the Council of Clermont, Pope Urban II announced the launch of the First Crusade. The aim was to capture Jerusalem permanently from the Muslims and to recover the Holy Land in the name of Christianity. People greeted the idea with great enthusiasm. The sources give information about the taking of Jerusalem in 1099 and the massacre of the inhabitants.

Source A: an extract from a modern textbook describing the attack on Jerusalem in 1099.

Once a section of the wall was captured, scaling ladders enabled many of the assailants [attackers] to climb into the city. The Crusaders, maddened by so great a victory after so much suffering, rushed through the streets and into the houses and mosques, killing all that they met, men, women and children alike.

Source B: an extract from William of Tyre, a twelfth-century writer who described the fall of Jerusalem.

The valiant Godfrey of Bouillon, the knights and other men-at-arms who were with him, descended from the walls, all armed, into the town. They went together through the streets with their swords in their hands. All them that they met, they slew and smote [cut] down, unarmed men, women and children, sparing none. They slew so many in the street that there were heaps of dead bodies. The foot-soldiers went to other parts of the town holding in their hands great poleaxes and other weapons, slaying all the Turks they could find. For they [the Turks] were people that our men had the greatest hatred for and so would gladly put them to death.

Source C: a nineteenth-century painting of the final capture of Jerusalem by the crusaders on 15 July 1099.

Question

Using **ALL** the sources and your own knowledge, is it true to say that the First Crusade achieved all its aims?

3 Richard the Lionheart

Read the introduction and the sources and then answer the question which follows.

→ ## Introduction

Richard the Lionheart was one of the most inspirational rulers of his day. As a warrior he was more than a match for Saladin. In the Holy Land, his siege craft at Acre drew the admiration of the other crusading commanders. Although in England for barely six months in his ten-year reign, the basic organisation of the country remained intact. Richard made careful arrangements for the administration of the kingdom during his absence and certain aspects of government, such as the keeping of written records, were improved.

Source A: an extract from a modern textbook describing some of the qualities of Richard I.

In the popular mind today, Richard is a national English hero, the fearless warrior and glorious crusader who struggled against all the odds to come within reach of capturing Jerusalem from the legendary Saladin on the Third Crusade. But, as king, he never spent more than six months in England. It has been argued by historians that Richard was an utterly irresponsible king who diverted the wealth of England to his own glory in France and the Holy Land and who recklessly endangered the security and stability of his island realm. But far from setting out on crusade without a care for the safety of his kingdom, Richard did what he could in the short time available to him. There now seems little doubt that he was one of the ablest men to have sat on the throne of England.

Source B: an extract from the Chronicle of Richard of Devizes, a twelfth-century Benedictine monk at Winchester. A well-informed author, he wrote enthusiastically about Richard I.

The time of commencing his journey pressed hard upon King Richard. He, who had been the first of all Princes on this side of the Alps in taking up of the cross, was unwilling to be the last in setting out. Richard was a king worthy of the name of king, who in the first year of his reign left the kingdom of England for Christ. So great was the devotion of the king that he speedily did run to avenge the wrongs of Christ. However, while he kept this great matter in his mind, he appointed the Bishop of Durham to be chief justice of the whole realm. The king then received security from the Welsh and the Scots that they would not pass their borders for the annoyance of England during his absence. In the year of the Lord, 1190, the King crossed the Channel to Neustria [Normandy], the care of the whole kingdom being committed to the Chancellor [William, Bishop of Ely].

Source C: a twentieth-century illustration of Richard the Lionheart fighting in the Third Crusade.

Question

Using **ALL** the sources and your own knowledge, is it true to say that Richard the Lionheart merely used England as a bank from which to take money to pay for all his foreign adventures?

4 Archbishop Becket

Read the introduction and the sources and then answer the question which follows.

→ Introduction

In 1162, Henry II appointed his close companion Thomas Becket as Archbishop of Canterbury. Henry wished to increase royal power over the Church, and thought that this would be easy with his friend as archbishop. But when Henry tried to press his claims, Becket resisted, championing the rights of the clergy against the king. Tension between the two increased, until Henry lost his patience. In desperation he yelled, 'Will no one rid me of this turbulent priest?' At this outburst, four of the king's knights took him at his word, rushing off to murder the archbishop.

Source A: an extract from a modern historian who describes how, when the knights approached him, Becket made no attempt to escape. The archbishop appeared to be expecting a violent death and almost seemed to welcome it.

There are indications that the prospect of being a martyr was not unwelcome to Becket. He resisted attempts to protect him from the knights and would take none of the possible opportunities to escape. When he entered the cathedral, the monks attempted to bolt the doors, but he ordered them to be thrown open. 'It is not proper to make a fortress of the house of prayer. We came to suffer, not to resist,' he said. Had he so wished, the archbishop might easily have saved himself by escape. The crypt was near at hand where there were many dark and winding passages. There was also another door near by, but none of these ways of escape would he take.

Source B: part of an eyewitness account by his biographer Edward Grim, of Becket's murder on 29 December 1170. This was published in about 1180. Grim, a Cambridge clerk on a visit to Canterbury, received a serious wound to his arm as he tried to protect the archbishop.

Without delay the godless men entered the house of peace with swords drawn. 'Where is Thomas Becket, traitor of the king and kingdom?' No one responded and instantly they cried out more loudly, 'Where is the archbishop?' 'Here I am, not a traitor of the king but a priest. Why do you seek me? Here, I am ready to suffer in the name of Him who redeemed me with His blood. God forbid that I should flee on account of your swords.' With rapid motion they laid hands on him. He bravely pushed one of the knights, who suddenly set upon him and sliced off the top of his head. Then, with another blow received on the head, Becket still remained firm. But with the third, the stricken martyr bent his knees and elbows, offering himself as a living sacrifice. But a fourth knight inflicted a grave wound and shattered his sword on the stone and his head, so that the blood turned white from the brains. A fifth man placed his foot on the neck of the holy priest and precious martyr and scattered the brains with the blood across the floor, exclaiming to the rest, 'We can leave this place, knights; he will not get up again!'

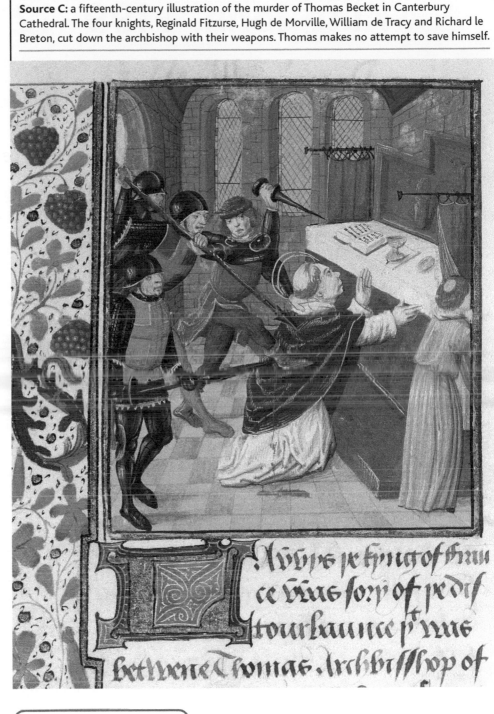

Source C: a fifteenth-century illustration of the murder of Thomas Becket in Canterbury Cathedral. The four knights, Reginald Fitzurse, Hugh de Morville, William de Tracy and Richard le Breton, cut down the archbishop with their weapons. Thomas makes no attempt to save himself.

Question

Using **ALL** the sources and your own knowledge, do you think that Thomas Becket caused his own death?

5 King John, 1199–1216

Read the introduction and the sources and then answer the question which follows.

→ ## Introduction

King John had a troubled reign. In 1204, he lost Normandy and soon afterwards, the rest of his French lands. He upset the Church and the Pope. Accused of seeking too much feudal power in his kingdom, John clashed with his barons who forced him to agree to *Magna Carta* in 1215. John is said to have been a tyrant and one of the worst of all English kings, who even secretly disposed of his nephew, Arthur, whom he saw as a threat to his position as king.

Source A: an extract from the Latin chronicler of the Cistercian abbey of Margam in Glamorgan, who wrote his narrative well after the event. He gives an account of the murder of Arthur, John's nephew.

After King John had captured Arthur and kept him alive in prison for some time, at length, in the castle of Rouen, after dinner on the Thursday before Easter [3 April 1203] when he was drunk and possessed by the devil, John slew him with his own hand, and tying a heavy stone to the body cast it into the River Seine. It was discovered by a fisherman in his net, and being dragged to the bank and recognised, it was taken for a secret burial, in fear of the tyrant, to the priory of Bec.

Source B: an extract from a modern writer commenting on John as a ruler.

John has often been regarded as a bad king, a thoroughly evil character, and one of the worst of all English sovereigns. At first, the case against him is strong. Even so, there is much more to be said in his defence than may be offered on behalf of several English monarchs who have enjoyed a better reputation. His were difficult, challenging times, during which there was heavy inflation; barons were increasingly reluctant to serve their king abroad; France was becoming stronger. If John reacted savagely to some of these problems, so too did other Medieval monarchs. John was at times an energetic and successful ruler, who developed the navy. He was also a hard-working administrator and judge.

Source C: a nineteenth-century illustration of King John signing *Magna Carta* at Runnymede on 15 June 1215 with the barons looking on carefully. The Charter was in part a reaction to some of John's failures and an attempt to restrain some aspects of royal power.

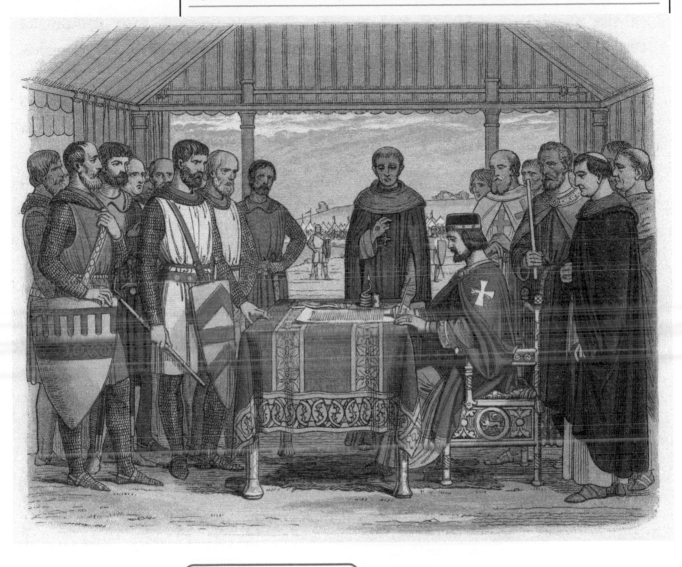

Question

Using **ALL** the sources and your own knowledge, how far is it true to say that John was a bad king?

The Black Death, 1348–50

Read the introduction and the sources and then answer the question which follows.

→ ## Introduction

The Black Death, or Bubonic Plague, was a disease that started in Asia. It spread westwards rapidly, reaching Europe in the 1340s and England by 1348. Between 1348 and 1350, about one-third of England's population died of this mysterious and unseen enemy. This resulted in a shortage of labour and demands from peasants for a rise in their wages. Many people also saw the plague as God's special punishment against the wickedness of the age.

Source A: an extract from the fourteenth-century chronicler, Henry Knighton, writing from his monastery in Leicester, about the causes of the Black Death. He sees the coming of plague as God's judgement for the sins of mankind.

In those days [1348] there arose a huge rumour and outcry among the people, because when tournaments were held, almost in every place, a band of women would come as if to share the sport, sometimes to the number of 40 or 50 ladies. There, they spent and lavished their possessions, and wearied their bodies with fooleries and wanton buffoonery. But God, in this matter as in all others, brought marvellous remedy. He harassed the places appointed for such vanities with rain and thunder and lightning and then came a general shower of death throughout the kingdom.

Source B: an extract from a modern historian describing some of the details of the Black Death and its effects.

When the plague arrived in 1348 no one knew what it was. Everyone was stunned. Men were said to fall down and die with only a glance from a victim. In no time the symptoms were familiar, boils which could be the size of an apple and black spots on the skin. Those who spat blood died in three days, the rest in five. The plague spared no one, rich or poor, clergy or laity. The population shrank and so did the amount of land under cultivation. At the same time, those who were left untouched could charge more for their work, so wages went up. So scarce was labour that at times livestock wandered in the fields, and at harvest-time the crops perished, for there was no one to bring them in.

Source C: a modern drawing of the effects of the Black Death showing villagers burying their dead. In some villages virtually the whole population was wiped out.

Question

Using **ALL** the sources and your own knowledge, do you agree that the effects of the plague were more than just social?

Henry V, 1413–22

Read the introduction and the sources and then answer the question which follows.

→ Introduction

From the moment he became king in 1413, Henry V was determined to win what he saw as his rightful lands in France. His military campaign began in August 1415 with the siege of Harfleur. He then won a glorious victory at Agincourt on 25 October. Further triumphs followed and the whole of Normandy was his by the beginning of 1419. However, after Henry V's death, the tide of war turned. By 1453, the English had been driven out of the whole of France apart from Calais. Victory at Agincourt seemed wasted.

Source A: a modern writer gives a clear opinion about the long-term results of the Battle of Agincourt and of Henry V's warlike policies in France.

Further successes followed Agincourt and the French asked for peace. By the Treaty of Troyes (1420), Charles VI agreed to disinherit his son and recognise Henry, married to his daughter Katherine, as 'heir to France'. On the surface of it, the king of England had restored his nation to glory. But it was merely a daydream. The greatest difficulty was that the treaty stated that Henry could be king of France, but he would have to pay for the conquest of it first. He returned to France in June 1422 to begin that long task which was cut short by his death on 31 August. In many ways if Henry V had not revived the war with France, he would have been a greater king. He had restored the fortunes of the monarchy, but his belief in his rights led him to take his country into a war which could never be won and he left his heir to face defeat.

Source B: an extract from an account of the Battle of Agincourt by Jean de Wavrin, the son of a Flemish knight. His father and older brother fought on the French side and were killed. The young de Wavrin observed the battle from the French lines.

Then the English archers saw that they were near enough and began to send their arrows on the French with great vigour. Then the French placed themselves together in order, everyone under his banner, their helmets on their heads. Thus they went forward a little, but before they could come to close quarters, many of the French were disabled and wounded by the arrows. When they came quite up to the English, they were so closely pressed one against another that none of them could lift their weapons to strike their enemies, except some that were in front. The French knights struck into these English archers, who had their stakes fixed in front of them. Their horses stumbled among the stakes, and they were speedily slain by the archers. Most of the rest, through fear, gave way and fell back.

Source C: a fifteenth-century illustration of the Battle of Agincourt, showing the fierce hand-to-hand fighting and the slaughter of many French knights. The main French attack was dismounted, although French cavalry on the wings of the battle-line suffered greatly as a hail of arrows from the longbowmen struck down both men and horses.

Question

Using **ALL** the sources and your own knowledge, do you agree that Henry's victory at Agincourt actually achieved very little?

Women in medieval society

Read the introduction and the sources and then answer the question which follows.

→ ## Introduction

During the Middle Ages, there were lots of restrictions on the daily lives of women. For instance, they could not sit in Parliament. They were not allowed into many professions, such as medicine. The law also put many limits on their rights so that, in effect, they were second-class citizens. On the other hand, some women, like Eleanor of Aquitaine or Matilda, gained great power. Others lived comfortably in nunneries or as the wives of noblemen, knights or rich merchants. For them life was easier than that of peasant women who often had to toil in the fields.

Source A: an extract from a modern historian describing the place of women in the medieval world.

After the Norman Conquest, women found their status reduced. In Anglo-Saxon England they had more or less enjoyed equality with men. That was now taken away and St. Paul's attitude to women, as being below men, became much more common. Women were subject first to their fathers and then, on marriage, to their husbands. Only when a woman became a wealthy widow did she gain any form of power or independence.

Source B: an extract from a fourteenth-century book advising noble women about their important duties concerning landed estates.

Some advice for ladies living in their castles, or on their estates. These women spend much of their lives in households without husbands. The men usually are at court or in distant countries. So the ladies will have the responsibilities for managing their property. A woman must know the yearly income from her estate. She should know how to manage accounts, in what season the fields should be fertilized and the best time for sowing. She must hire good labourers. She will insist that they get up early, and will rise early herself, put on a cloak, go to the window and watch there until she sees them go out, for labourers are usually inclined to laziness.

Source C: a fourteenth-century illustration showing women spinning and carding wool. English wool was the finest in Europe and large quantities were exported to the cloth-making areas of Flanders and northern Italy. Wool was the basis of much of England's wealth. Women played an important role in its production.

Question

Using **ALL** the sources and your own knowledge, how far do you agree that medieval women were unimportant?

9 Richard III, 1483–85

Read the introduction and the sources and then answer the question which follows.

→ Introduction

After his defeat and death at the Battle of Bosworth in 1485, Tudor historians began to destroy the reputation of Richard III. Attitudes to Richard were then confirmed by William Shakespeare, who portrayed the king as the personification of evil in his play *Richard III*. Richard has been accused of murdering his way to a throne that was not rightfully his. He then reigned for two years in a climate of crisis, violence and injustice. Despite this, Richard was a fine soldier. He had remained loyal to his brother, Edward IV, during the Wars of the Roses, fighting bravely by his side at the battles of Barnet and Tewkesbury in 1471.

Source A: an extract from the *Anglica Historia* [History of England] by Polydore Vergil. This work was first published around 1535 and its view of many events was shaped by Henry VII.

When his brother King Edward departed his life, Duke Richard of Gloucester was in Yorkshire, and William Hastings, the Chamberlain, sent him trusty messengers with a letter to inform him of his brother's death. William urged him to go as soon as possible to fetch Prince Edward and bring him to London, so as to take up the government. When Richard learned this, he immediately began to burn with desire for the crown. Having nothing but cruel and savage things in mind, he transferred his nephews to the Tower. Then he wrote a letter to Robert Brackenbury, the Governor of the Tower, commanding him to find some way of quickly killing his nephews. But the Governor, when he received the king's horrid instructions, was astonished at the atrocity of the thing. The king then compelled James Tyrell to do the deed. Tyrell went to London and killed the royal children, setting an example nearly unheard-of within human memory. Thus Prince Edward died, together with his brother Richard, but it is unknown what manner of death the poor little boys suffered.

Source B: an extract from a modern writer discussing the character and achievements of Richard III.

Richard is one of England's most controversial figures. In April 1483, his future was put in doubt by the death of his brother. Through a series of masterstrokes, Richard seized power. In June, he made himself king. Loyal to Edward IV before 1483, he is seen by many to have devoted his energies to the well-being of the north. But it has also been argued that he was single-mindedly pursuing his own power. Above all, comes the debate over his crimes. He is probably to be found not guilty of the murder of Edward [son of Henry VI] at Tewkesbury, of organising the destruction of Clarence [younger brother of Edward IV], or of poisoning his queen. He was probably associated with the murder of Henry VI. His guilt is not certain on the princes in the Tower.

Source C: a nineteenth-century illustration of the murder of the Princes in the Tower in 1483 on the orders of their uncle Richard. Their deaths removed an important threat to his kingship. Shakespeare called these murders a 'tyrannous and bloody act'.

Question

Using **ALL** the sources and your own knowledge, should Richard III be seen as anything more than a cruel and ruthless usurper?

EVIDENCE QUESTIONS
THE MAKING OF THE UNITED
KINGDOM:
1485–1750

10 Henry VII, 1485–1509

Read the introduction and the sources and then answer the question which follows.

→ ## Introduction

Henry VII was the first Tudor king. He came to the throne after a time of great unrest and he had to re-establish peace in England as well as strengthen his own claim to the throne. In order to achieve this, he crushed rebellions and controlled his over-mighty subjects. He also needed to build up trade and strengthen the law. The maintenance of England's interests in Europe was another of his major undertakings. But Henry also understood the power of wealth and at his death there was plenty of money in the royal treasury.

Source A: an extract from the *Anglica Historia* [History of England] by Polydore Vergil, first published around 1535. Although Vergil wrote several years after the king's death, he had certainly met and talked with Henry. He provides probably the fullest description of the sort of man the king was.

His body was slender but well built and strong; his height above the average. His face was cheerful, especially when speaking and his eyes were small and blue. He was distinguished, wise and prudent in character and his mind was brave and resolute. In government he was shrewd. No one got the better of him by deceit or dishonest practice. He was most fortunate in war, but, by nature, he preferred peace. Above all things, he valued justice. He was a most passionate supporter of the Church and daily took part in religious services. But in his later days, all these virtues were obscured by greed for money. In a monarch, this is the worst of all vices, since it hurts everyone and upsets those qualities of trust, justice and honesty with which a kingdom should be governed.

Source B: an extract from a twentieth-century historian summing up the character and achievements of Henry VII by 1509.

The main rebels were ruined or dead. Restless Ireland was in good order, warlike Scotland had made peace. The valuable trade of the Netherlands had been secured by the Magnus Intercursus and useful trade treaties had been made with other countries. Marriage arrangements had been made with Spain, mighty France was friendly. Henry stood before the eyes of Europe as a king whose title was firmly established and whose power was considerable. After the death of his wife [1503] he gave way to the sin of avarice. Yet he had great qualities. He revived the strength of the English monarchy and set it along the path to future greatness. He has some claim to be regarded as the greatest of Tudors.

Source C: a page from the royal accounts of Henry VII. Payments to various people are shown. Henry did not like to part with his money, so he carefully checked all outgoings before signing the sheet. His initials may be seen at the bottom right-hand-side of the page.

Question

Using **ALL** the sources and your own knowledge, should Henry VII be remembered merely as a greedy king?

11 Henry VIII and Anne Boleyn

Read the introduction and the sources and then answer the question which follows.

→ ## Introduction

After receiving special permission from Pope Julius II, Henry VIII had married Catherine of Aragon in 1509. She had been married previously to Henry's elder brother, Arthur, who had died in 1502. By 1525 Catherine had still not produced a son and heir, and now Henry was growing desperate. He was also turning his attention to a new lady at his court, Anne Boleyn.

Source A: an extract from a twentieth-century textbook about Henry VIII's marriage situation with Catherine of Aragon in 1527. For some years, Catherine had been under pressure to produce a son. Of her seven children, only a daughter, Mary, had survived.

In 1527 Henry's queen was forty and past having children. Her only surviving child was one sickly daughter, Mary. Henry saw that as a judgement for marrying his brother's widow. Henry wanted a son and he was now deeply in love with a lady of the court, Anne Boleyn, young enough to have children. Anne was an ambitious, educated woman. Wolsey's task was to obtain a divorce from the pope, so that the king could marry. This he failed to do. The king was furious.

Source B: A letter from Henry VIII to Anne Boleyn written in 1527. By this date, Henry was passionately in love with Anne although he admired other ladies as well! Ever aware of the symbols of love, in the previous year Henry had ordered from his goldsmith some brooches as gifts for Anne. One represented Venus and Cupid, the Roman goddess and god of love, while the second showed a lady holding a heart in her hand.

I ask you with a full heart to tell me clearly what opinion you have of the love between us. For I absolutely must have an answer of this sort, for I have been pierced with the arrow of love for more than a year now, and do not know whether I am doomed or have found a place in your heart and your strong affection. If you mean to take the place of a true, faithful Mistress and friend and to give yourself with body and soul to him who wants to be your true servant (unless you strictly forbid it), then I promise you that I will put all others who are about you out of my thoughts, and serve only you. I ask you to give me a full response to this rude [rough, clumsy,] letter, saying what I can expect. And if you do not want to answer me in a letter, tell me a place where I can hear it from your mouth – I will be there with a joyful heart.

Henry Rex [King]

Source C: a nineteenth-century French painting showing Cranmer telling Catherine that she was to be divorced from Henry VIII. By 1533, events had moved quickly. Despite consideration by the Church courts, the 'Great Matter' was not settled. Then Anne was found to be pregnant, so Henry married her in January of that year. Catherine had to go.

Question

Using **ALL** the sources and your own knowledge, is it true to say that Henry VIII divorced Catherine of Aragon only because he wanted an heir to the throne?

12 Henry VIII and the English Reformation, 1529–40

Read the introduction and the sources and then answer the question which follows.

→ Introduction

One important element of the English Reformation was the Dissolution of the Monasteries (1536–40). Over the centuries monasteries had become rich, owning vast amounts of land, property, gold and silver plate and other precious treasures. Henry VIII was desperate for money, and the monasteries had plenty, so dissolving them was an easy solution to one of his most pressing problems. Although financial need played a huge part in Henry's religious changes at the Reformation, it was just one of many other causes.

Source A: an extract from a letter of Richard Layton to Thomas Cromwell, dated 22 September 1539. Layton was one of three visitors sent to examine the abbot during Glastonbury Abbey's closure. This was one of the largest and richest monasteries in England. The abbey was searched and stripped of valuable items. Richard Whiting, the abbot, was sent to the Tower. Later found guilty of treason, he was hanged, drawn and quartered on a hill near his old abbey.

Your lordship, we came to Glastonbury on Friday last past, about ten o'clock in the forenoon and because the abbot was then at Sharpham, a place of his, a mile or more from the abbey, we, without any delay, went into the same place, and there examined him. And because his answer was not then to our liking, we advised him to remember that which he had forgotten, and so declare the truth. We proceeded that night to search his study for letters and books and found a written book of arguments against the divorce of his king's majesty. And so we proceeded again to his examination. We have in money £300, as well as a large quantity of plate and other stuff. We have found a fair chalice of gold, and several other pieces of plate, which the abbot had secretly hid.

Source B: an extract from a modern writer discussing the various factors which led to the English Reformation under Henry VIII.

By the time Henry VIII wanted his divorce from Catherine of Aragon, reforming, Protestant ideas were already well established in Germany under the leadership of Martin Luther. These ideas were slowly reaching England. Events took a sharp turn with the summoning of Parliament in November 1529. The Commons were envious of the wealth of the Church, which held about one third of all the country's land. They resented paying tithes and hated church courts. They were disgusted at the corruption and worldliness of many of the clergy. So the scene was set for acts which were to bring about the greatest changes to England since 1066.

Source C: an illustration from the early twentieth century showing Cromwell's men smashing a shrine in a monastery. All treasures were noted and sent to the king's agents. Items of gold and silver were melted down. Money was carefully counted and coins weighed.

Question

Using **ALL** the sources and your own knowledge, how far is it true to say that Henry's desire for wealth was the main cause of the English Reformation?

13 Mary I and Lady Jane Grey

Read the introduction and the sources and then answer the question which follows.

→ Introduction

On 10 July 1553, it was announced that Jane Grey would be queen. Hearing this, Mary wrote to the Council claiming the throne, gathered her followers and marched on London. With Mary's support increasing, Jane Grey's father, the Duke of Suffolk, tore down the canopy of state hanging above her throne, telling his daughter that her short reign was over. At first, Mary showed mercy to many of those who had plotted against her, but after Wyatt's Rebellion (January–February 1554) she took a tough line against her political or religious enemies.

Source A: an extract from a modern historian describing Mary's attitude to those who had opposed her in Wyatt's Rebellion. There were many executions, but mercy, too, was shown to some.

As a London diarist recorded, 'some of the men of Kent went to the court with nooses about their necks. The poor prisoners knelt down in the mud, and there, the Queen looked out over the gate and gave them all pardon and they cried out, "God save Queen Mary!" as they went'. Mary's victory was secure. Five days after Wyatt's surrender, Lady Jane Grey and her husband were put to death. Both had been found guilty of high treason and condemned in November 1553. Then, Mary had maintained Jane's innocence and said that her conscience would not allow her to have Jane executed. But now, the involvement of Jane's father in Wyatt's rebellion sealed his daughter's fate. Although Jane and her husband had taken no part in it, they now represented too great a threat to live.

Source B: part of a letter to the Marquis of Northampton written on 11 July 1553 by Lady Jane Grey as Queen. She writes announcing her succession and ordering certain measures to be taken to secure her possession of the crown.

From Jane, the Queen: Right trusty and well beloved Cousin, we greet you well. Whereas it hath pleased Almighty God to call out of this life, King Edward, we are entered into our rightful possession of the Kingdom. As agreed by the last will of the old King, signed with his own hand and sealed with the Great Seal of the Kingdom. To which the Nobles of this Realm and all our Council and Judges with the Mayor and Chief Councillors of the City of London, have also subscribed their names. We do this day make our entry into our Tower of London as Rightful Queen of this Realm. We have set forth our commands to all our loving subjects, telling them all their duties of obedience which they owe to us. We command you to defend our just title and to assist us in the rightful possession of this Kingdom and to repel and resist the false and untrue claim of the Lady Mary.

Source C: a nineteenth-century illustration showing Lady Jane Grey on her way to her execution on the morning of 12 February 1554. She denied any involvement in Wyatt's Rebellion, but confessed her guilt for involvement in Northumberland's political schemes. She was just seventeen, but a political threat to Mary.

Question

Using **ALL** the sources and your own knowledge, how far do you agree that Mary I was right to execute Lady Jane Grey?

Mary I

Read the introduction and the sources and then answer the question which follows.

→ Introduction

Mary Tudor was a devout Catholic. On coming to the throne in 1553, her main mission was to make England a Roman Catholic country again and to undo all the work of Edward VI and Henry VIII. By so doing, Mary believed she was saving her country from deadly sin. She was even ready to use force if necessary. Although religion dominated her mind, Mary had to deal with all aspects of government at home, as well as managing her foreign policy.

Source A: an extract from a modern author making some final judgements about Mary I and her reign.

Mary resolutely believed that there was only one way to Heaven and that was through strictly following the teachings of the Roman Catholic Church. No other way would do. There could be no deviation from Roman Catholic beliefs without risking the dangers of Hell. Enforcing her wishes on her people led Mary to be cruel. But the queen must be given credit for courageously sticking to her religious principles. Mary also tried to improve her realm. Government institutions evolved steadily; there was planned reform of the coinage; trade was encouraged both at home and abroad and proposals for a better navy were devised. On the other hand, at her death, Mary had no husband beside her and no Roman Catholic heir. Her foreign policy had failed and she had lost Calais. Furthermore, the fires of Smithfield had led to popular hatred of the very religion Mary had championed so valiantly.

Source B: an extract from John Foxe's *Book of Martyrs*, published in 1563 to glorify the Protestant martyrs. This piece describes the death of Thomas Cranmer, Archbishop of Canterbury (1533–56), who finally decided to oppose Mary and remain a Protestant.

Then the Spanish friar, John, began to exhort him [press him to turn Catholic] but Cranmer bid him farewell. Then was an iron chain tied about Cranmer and when the wood was kindled and the fire began to burn near him, he put his right hand into the flame, which he held so steadfast and immovable, that all men might see his hand burnt before his body was touched. His eyes were lifted up to heaven. He repeated the words 'Lord Jesus, receive my spirit' and in the greatness of the flames, he gave up the ghost.

Source C: an eighteenth-century engraving showing the burning of Protestant martyrs in Smithfield, London. People were sometimes burned in groups as well as on their own. Their sufferings were often made to look as shocking as possible.

The Martyrdom of T.Losby, H.Ramsey, T.Thirtell, Marg! Hide, and Agnes Stanley, in Smithfield.

Question

Using **ALL** the sources and your own knowledge, was Mary I a cruel queen who failed in everything she tried to do?

15 Elizabeth I and Mary Stuart

Read the introduction and the sources and then answer the question which follows.

→ Introduction

After her defeat at the Battle of Langside in May 1568, Mary Stuart fled for protection to England, throwing herself on the mercy of her cousin, Elizabeth I. She was kept in captivity for nineteen years, being constantly moved from place to place. But she was implicated in a number of Roman Catholic plots to overthrow Elizabeth, and was increasingly seen both as a political and religious threat to the queen's safety. Elizabeth's chief ministers, Burghley and Walsingham, wanted Mary dead. After the scare of the Babington Plot in 1586, Mary was put on trial, found guilty and sentenced to death. Despite Elizabeth's initial reluctance, Mary was beheaded at Fotheringhay Castle on 8 February 1587.

Source A: at the opening of the trial of Mary, Queen of Scots, at Fotheringhay in October 1586, the Commissioners delivered her this personal letter from Queen Elizabeth. It has been translated from the French.

You have in various ways and manners attempted to take my life and to bring my kingdom to destruction by bloodshed. I have never proceeded so harshly against you, but have, on the contrary, protected and maintained you like myself. These treasons will be proved to you and all will be made clear. It is now my will, that you answer the nobles and peers of the kingdom as if I were myself present. I therefore require, charge, and command that you make answer, for I have been well informed of your arrogance. Act plainly without reserve, and you will sooner be able to obtain favour of me.

Source B: an extract from a twentieth-century history book discussing the threat that Mary, Queen of Scots, posed to England and to Elizabeth.

Mary was still in a position to make trouble for Elizabeth. Since the Throckmorton Plot (1583) her freedom to use money from France to pay her agents and to keep constantly in touch with Paris and Edinburgh had been reduced. But she was still, by her very own existence, able to endanger that of the queen. 'So long as that devilish woman lives', wrote Walsingham, 'neither can her majesty continue in quiet enjoyment of her crown, nor her faithful servants assure themselves of the safety of their lives.' It had long been understood that Elizabeth's death was necessary for any successful rebellion or invasion that might be launched to place Mary on the throne. The problems of the queen's security were constantly discussed by her Councillors.

Source C: an early twentieth-century illustration showing Elizabeth I in 1587, hesitating to sign the warrant for the execution of her cousin, Mary, Queen of Scots, despite pressure from Lord Burghley, her chief minister.

Question

Using **ALL** the sources and your own knowledge, do you think that Elizabeth I was right to execute Mary?

16 The causes of the English Civil War, 1629–42

Read the introduction and the sources and then answer the question which follows.

→ Introduction

A significant move toward Civil War in England occurred when the House of Commons, led by John Pym, turned against Charles I's two chief ministers, William Laud and the Earl of Strafford, mainly on account of their work in government and the Church during the period of Personal Rule, 1629–40. Tensions increased and there was a breakdown between King and Parliament. In November 1640 the two royal ministers were sent to the Tower accused of treason. Both were later executed.

Source A: an extract from an oath of 1640 which Archbishop Laud required to be taken by all clergy and schoolmasters. The administration of the oath was to be overseen by each bishop in his diocese. This naturally created opposition to Laud and the government from Roman Catholics and Puritans.

I, ..., do swear that I do approve the doctrine and government established in the Church of England, as containing all things necessary to salvation. And that I will not attempt to bring in any Popish doctrine [religious ideas]. Nor will I ever agree to alter the government of the Church by archbishops, bishops and deans, as it stands now established. And all these things I do acknowledge and sincerely swear according to the plain common sense of these words without any mental reservations or secrets. And this I do willingly and truly, upon the faith of a Christian. So help me God, in Jesus Christ.

Source B: an extract from a modern history book discussing the destruction of the machinery of Personal Rule by the Long Parliament. Such laws were largely the work of radical parliamentary leaders such as John Pym and John Hampden, who pressed hard to reduce royal power. This naturally created opposition to Parliament from Royalists.

A series of Acts was also passed in the summer of 1641, which went a good deal further than merely attacking the royal abuses of the 1630s, or Charles's Personal Rule. These destroyed the very institutions of traditional government. They included the abolition of Star Chamber and the Court of High Commission. These measures were far reaching. Not only did they ensure that kingship without parliament could not be repeated, but also that the whole machinery of Divine Right Kingship could not be revived. Many in parliament wished to limit the king's powers, particularly his free choice of ministers.

Source C: a seventeenth-century engraving showing the execution of the Earl of Strafford on Tower Hill, 12 May 1641. Strafford had faithfully served Charles I during the period of Personal Rule. Much of his power was exercised through the Court of Star Chamber.

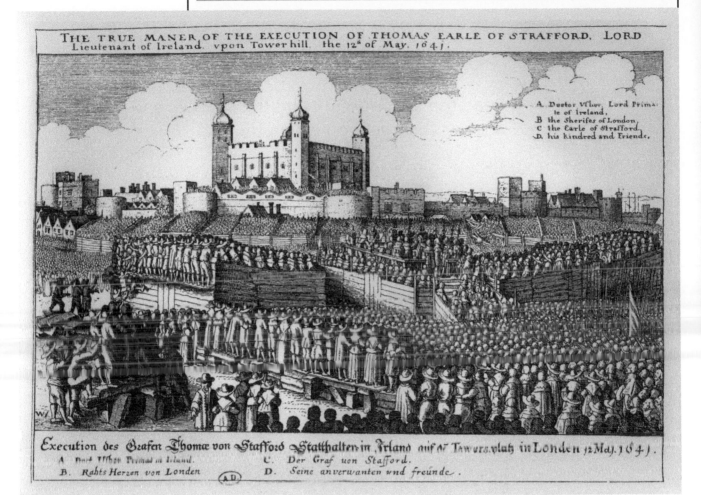

Question

Using **ALL** the sources and your own knowledge, do you agree that the English Civil War was caused largely by the actions of royal ministers and parliamentary leaders?

17 The execution of Charles I

Read the introduction and the sources and then answer the question which follows.

→ ## Introduction

Charles I had declared war on his Parliament in August 1642. After a series of military defeats, he was put on trial in January 1649, accused of being 'a tyrant, traitor and murderer, and a public and implacable [inflexible, stubborn] enemy to the Commonwealth of England'. He was found guilty and executed in London.

Source A: an account of the execution of Charles I from a modern textbook.

On Tuesday, 30 January 1649, Charles I was brought to his own Banqueting Hall in Whitehall, London. It was a gloomy, cold day, white with frost and snow. A procession of soldiers with beating drums escorted him to the black-draped scaffold. Charles's executioners wore disguises – masks and false beards. The king spoke to the people saying that he desired their liberty and freedom, ideas for which he believed he was dying. He then stripped off his jewels and his outer clothing. The block was low so he was forced to lie flat to put his head on it. He gave a signal to the executioner. The axe swung down, cutting off his head at one blow. The head was held up to the crowd, but only a few managed to dip their handkerchiefs in the royal blood which dripped from the scaffold.

Source B: an extract from *The History of England* by Laurence Echard, a Lincolnshire cleric writing in 1720. Here, he describes Charles I's execution and people's reactions to it.

His head was at one blow severed from his body. None of the kings of England ever left this World with more open marks of sorrow and affection. The Venerable Archbishop Usher swooned [fainted] at the sight of the fatal blow, as at an event too great for Heaven to permit, or the Earth to behold. As the rumours of the king's death spread throughout the kingdom, many of both sexes fell into palpitations, swooning and melancholy [sadness] and some, with a sudden upset, died.

Source C: this eighteenth-century engraving, based on a contemporary drawing, shows the scene of the execution of Charles I. The king's head has just been cut off and is being held up by the executioner. Large crowds turned out to watch and many people even climbed onto the roof of the Banqueting House. At the moment of the king's death, the people let out a huge groan.

Question

Using **ALL** the sources and your own knowledge, how far do you agree that Charles I was a hated tyrant and traitor who deserved to die in 1649?

18 The Plague of London, 1665

Read the introduction and the sources and then answer the question which follows.

→ Introduction

A great outbreak of bubonic plague swept into London in the spring of 1665. This disease was carried by fleas on the back of the black rat. Doctors, however, were helpless as they really did not understand what caused the illness. When the plague died down about 100,000 people, or one-quarter of London's population, had lost their lives.

Source A: an extract from a modern historian giving some explanations for the spread of the Great Plague.

Medical science was still primitive, so there was little awareness of hygiene. Through the City ran an open sewer called the Fleet Ditch. Although it was realised that some animals carried the Plague, the offending rats do not seem to have been feared. Superstition was almost as common as the disease itself. Pepys would sometimes wear a hare's foot around his neck, hoping it would keep the sickness away. Some said that the disaster was happening because the next year, 1666, was unlucky (three sixes being particularly devilish). Astrologers said that the true cause was connected with the position of the planets. Religious people regarded the outbreak as a judgement from God for the sins of the king's Court.

Source B: an extract from an account of the Plague by Nathaniel Hodges. Hodges was a London doctor in 1665. He treated patients as well as he could. His writings list both the symptoms and recommended cures for the disease. In this passage, he describes the precautions taken by the City authorities to stop the spread of the disease.

An order was immediately issued to shut up all the infected houses. A law was made for marking the houses of infected persons with a red cross, having with it, LORD HAVE MERCY UPON US, and that a guard should wait there continually, both to hand to the sick the necessary food and medicines and to prevent them from coming out of their houses until forty days after their recovery.

But although the Lord Mayor carried out these orders, yet it was to no purpose, for the plague more and more increased. There were monthly Publick Prayers to soothe the anger of Heaven. His majesty commanded the College of Physicians to visit infected people on all occasions, but the disease was no sooner stifled in one family, but it broke out in many more. The authorities also ordered fires in the streets to purify the air.

Source C: a nineteenth-century engraving showing a London street during the Plague. The houses are packed together; a body lies unattended and a sewage channel runs down the middle of the roadway.

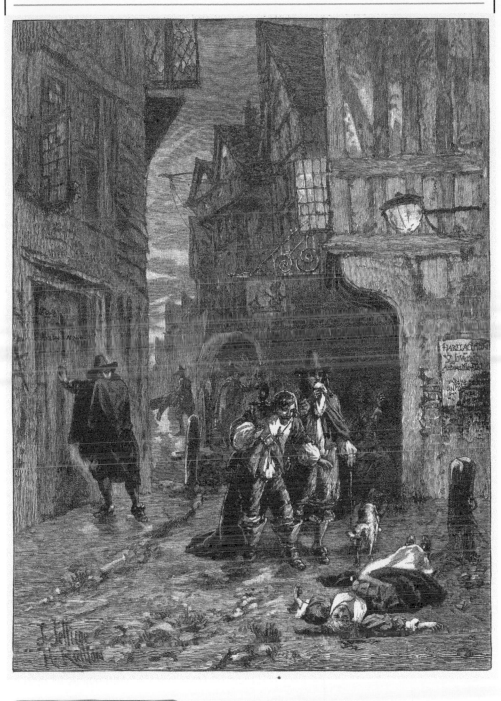

Question

Using **ALL** the sources and your own knowledge, how true is it to say that the spread of the Great Plague in London was caused by a lack of proper medical knowledge?

19 The Fire of London, 1666

Read the introduction and the sources and then answer the question which follows.

→ Introduction

The Great Fire of London began in the early hours of Sunday 2 September 1666 in the shop of Thomas Farynor, a baker in Pudding Lane. A strong east wind fanned the flames across the city. The blaze consumed Old St Paul's, the Guildhall, the Royal Exchange, Newgate Prison, the Old Bailey and the halls of the City Companies, together with 87 parish churches and more than 13,000 houses. Despite all the destruction and the social and economic hardships, the disaster nonetheless presented opportunities for improving England's capital.

Source A: a modern historian comments on the reconstruction of London after the fire.

Only a few days after the Great Fire, Sir Christopher Wren produced a plan for a new city. His ambitious scheme would have made London one of the wonders of the world. But Wren's wide streets and squares remained a dream. Despite this, Wren built at least 60 new churches and a tall column to commemorate the Fire. Wren's most famous task began in 1673, when the king ordered him to prepare plans for a new St Paul's. Most of the new buildings, though, were ordinary houses. The Rebuilding Act (1667) achieved a lasting improvement in the fabric of London. To prevent fires, the new houses were to be faced in brick. Moreover, they were classified by size and were regulated according to the width of the street on to which they faced.

Source B: from the diary of John Evelyn who lived in London and witnessed the burning of the city 'with all the sky of a fiery aspect'. He describes the devastation as he walked about among the ruins on the morning of Friday 7 September.

I went this morning on foot from Whitehall as far as London Bridge, with extraordinary difficulty, clambering over heaps of still smoking rubbish and frequently mistaking where I was. The ground under my feet so hot, that it burnt the soles of my shoes. I was infinitely concerned to find St Paul's now a sad ruin. The lead, iron-work, bells and plate all melted; the Companies' Halls, splendid buildings, all in dust. The fountains dried up and former warehouses still burning in dark clouds of smoke. The people, who walked about the ruins, appeared like men in some dismal desert, or rather in some city, laid waste by a cruel enemy. The poor inhabitants were spread in St George's Fields and Moorfields, some under tents, some under miserable huts, and many without a rag.

Source C: a seventeenth-century Dutch painting showing the destruction in London by the Great Fire. In the words of Samuel Pepys there was 'an entire arch of fire above a mile long; the churches, houses all on fire and flaming at once'. The blaze laid waste 463 acres, which represented more than 80 per cent of the City within the walls.

Question

Using **ALL** the sources and your own knowledge, how far was the Great Fire of 1666 a total disaster for London?

20 John Churchill, Duke of Marlborough

Read the introduction and the sources and then answer the question which follows.

→ ## Introduction

In 1702, John Churchill, Duke of Marlborough, was appointed Commander-in-Chief of the Allied forces at the start of the War of the Spanish Succession. Despite its name, this was largely a conflict directed at the growing power of France under Louis XIV. In 1713, England emerged from Marlborough's war as a major European player and the world's greatest sea power. On the victorious battlefields of Blenheim, Ramilles, Oudenard and Malplaquet, Marlborough launched England into greatness. For France, the Treaty of Utrecht marked the end of her ambition to dominate Europe.

Source A: an extract from a modern historian describing some results of Marlborough's victory at the Battle of Blenheim on 13 August 1704. Marlborough had marched his troops down the Rhine to meet his ally, Eugène of Savoy. Together they gave battle to the French and won a resounding victory.

Marlborough was the architect of his first great battle, Blenheim. There, he secured a decisive victory for democracy. He saved the Hapsburg dynasty and humbled Louis XIV's Bourbon line. He handed England military greatness in Europe and destroyed the notion of French invincibility. The future of the United Provinces was guaranteed, while Bavaria was punished for her leader's treachery. Blenheim was the justification of William III's opinion; Louis XIV must be, and could be, stopped.

Source B: an extract from the journal of Sergeant Millner, a soldier in Marlborough's army. He was present at the battle, although his *Journal of all the Marches and Famous Battles* was not published until 1733. Here, he comments on the effect of Marlborough's victory at Blenheim on French morale.

The French Armies' former fiery Courage daily dwindled and they were quite disheartened. They still retained a Fear of being beaten by our worthy Hero [Marlborough] and our courageous and victorious Army wherever they met. This, accordingly, is what happened all along everywhere. So our Men were filled with Hope that wherever they met the French, they would beat them. So that during the War, the grand Allied Armies remained the Conquerors, and the French the conquered.

Source C: an eighteenth-century painting of the battle of Blenheim. Tallard, the captured French commander, is just leaving in Marlborough's coach. The French and Bavarians lost some 40,000 men: killed, wounded or captured. The taking of 129 colours and 110 standards reflected the greatness of Marlborough's victory.

Question

Using **ALL** the sources and your own knowledge, how important was the Battle of Blenheim in the War of the Spanish Succession?

21 The Jacobite Rebellion, 1745

Read the introduction and the sources and then answer the question which follows.

→ Introduction

In July 1745, Prince Charles Edward Stuart landed at Eriskay in the Western Isles with a few faithful companions. He raised his standard at Glenfinnan on 19 August. By then he had gathered over 900 men and support was growing. Then came his victory at Prestonpans in September. The Prince's aim was to establish his power in Scotland before marching into England to take the throne from George II. The English government was quite unprepared. The king himself was in Hanover and many of his troops were engaged abroad. To many, the Jacobites seemed threatening.

Source A: an extract from a modern historian commenting on the extent of the Jacobite threat during the rebellion.

Much of the momentum of the '45 came out of the sheer personal magnetism of the Young Pretender and his wild gambles and by the promise of the French to offer help. Indeed, the rising came astonishingly close to success even though the political climate was unfavourable. Fatally, the inability of the Jacobites to match their rising with French support in the end destroyed its prospects. The reluctance of the English, in particular, Roman Catholics, to support the uprising, doomed the rebellion to failure. A series of towns – Edinburgh, Carlisle, Lancaster, Preston and Derby – fell to the rebels without resistance, but it was up to the Jacobites to force their case. In the absence of a French invasion force in the south of England, they were unable to do so.

Source B: part of a letter to a friend written by Horace Walpole from his London home in December 1745, commenting on the progress of the Jacobite rebels.

The rebels marched in all haste to Derby. The news of this threw the whole town into great panic. They got nine thousand pounds at Derby. Then they retreated a few miles, but returned again to Derby, got ten thousand pounds more, plundered the town and burnt a house of the Countess of Exeter. Now, they are gone again, and it is said, have left all their cannon behind them and twenty wagons of sick men. The Duke of Cumberland has sent General Hawley to harass them in their retreat. They must either go to North Wales, where they will probably all perish, or to Scotland, with great loss. We dread them no longer.

Source C: a nineteenth-century view of the Highland Charge at the Battle of Prestonpans. This was an important Jacobite victory. Sir John Cope, commanding George II's forces, was beaten in this battle which lasted little more than five minutes. The victory brought Charles Edward many new recruits and, by the end of October, he was ready to invade England with a force of 4,500 infantry and 400 horsemen.

Question

Using **ALL** the sources and your own knowledge, how far do you consider the Jacobite Rebellion of 1745 a real threat to George II and his government?

EVIDENCE QUESTIONS
BRITAIN AND EMPIRE:
1750–1914

22 The causes of the American War of Independence, 1763–76

Read the introduction and the sources and then answer the question which follows.

→ ## Introduction

The declaration of American Independence, on 4 July 1776, meant that Britain had to go to war to defend what she saw as a violation of her right to rule her colonies. The outbreak of war ended a period of growing tension caused by a series of measures to tax and regulate colonial trade. American protests grew, resulting in unrest, riots, bloodshed and finally, war. However, when conflict came in 1775, it was for many more reasons than the idea of 'No Taxation without Representation'.

Source A: an extract from a twentieth-century American historian commenting on the overarching causes of the war in 1775.

There may still be some who labour under the impression that the American revolutionary movement was caused simply by the deeds of particular men such as Samuel Adams on the one hand and George III and George Grenville, on the other. But the break in the old British Empire did not come about by the actions of wicked men. It had its source in the fact that America now had a mature and powerful English-speaking community with a mind of its own and a future that it wanted to manage itself. The repressive actions of the British government generated a unity of action among the colonists; a unity strong enough to achieve political and religious independence and to lay the foundations for a great nation.

Source B: part of a speech by Samuel Adams, delivered to the State House in Philadelphia in August 1776. Adams was one of several thinkers and writers like Thomas Paine and Thomas Jefferson, who championed a new form of government for the Americans without British domination. Ideas such as these inevitably helped bring about war in 1775.

No man once had a greater respect for Englishmen than I. They were as dear to me as branches of the same parental trunk. But when I am aroused by the din of arms, Heaven forgive me if I cannot root out those passions which are implanted in my bosom. I detest submission to a people who have ceased to be human. Has Britain a single eye to our advantage? A nation of shopkeepers is very seldom so interested. Britain has treated us as beasts of burden. Courage, then, my countrymen! From the day on which any agreement takes place between Great Britain and America, on any other terms than as independent States, I shall date this day the ruin of this country. To unite the supremacy of Great Britain and the liberty of America is utterly impossible. We have no other alternative but independence. If I have a wish dearest to my soul, it is that these American States may never cease to be free and independent.

Source C: a modern engraving of the Boston Tea Party, 16 December 1773. This was a protest against the enforced import of cheap tea by the East India Company. The Sons of Liberty in Boston saw it as an attempt to raise an extra import duty. They dumped 300 chests of tea into the harbour, an action which spread to other colonies and provoked the English government to pass the Intolerable Acts of 1774.

Question

Using **ALL** the sources and your own knowledge, how far is it true to say that American opposition to British taxation was the main cause of the American War of Independence?

23 The Transport Revolution

Read the introduction and the sources and then answer the question which follows.

→ Introduction

From the mid-eighteenth century, transport improved dramatically. Better roads were developed through turnpike trusts and the work of individuals such as Thomas Telford and John Metcalf. A network of canals grew up. Railways expanded rapidly to link all major cities. Easier transportation of goods to the ports generated notable developments in shipping, as sail gave way to steam. By 1900, the British merchant fleet was twice the size of those of the USA and Germany combined. However, not everyone welcomed this Transport Revolution.

Source A: an extract from a modern historian writing about the mixed benefits of railway expansion. By 1880, the railway network, with more than 15,500 miles of track, handled 597 million passenger journeys and 232 million tons of freight. But for some, the coming of the Railway Age meant economic ruin.

Railway development was rapid, though opposed by many landowners and by the canal companies, who resented the loss of business. The Duke of Wellington had objected because he believed railways would encourage the lower classes to move about. This they certainly did and the availability of cheap travel contributed to major social change. Mail coaches were gradually withdrawn from service and the great highways of the eighteenth century became deserted, their posting inns falling on hard times and their toll gates left unattended. Manufacturers and traders, however, welcomed this new form of quick, reliable transport. The arrival of railways stimulated urban growth, often reviving trade in decaying medieval towns. There were new inland river ports like Gloucester and new railway centres such as Swindon. Commuter towns around London expanded, as did seaside resorts like Blackpool, Scarborough and Bournemouth.

Source B: an extract from the Prospectus of the Liverpool and Manchester Railway, written in October 1824 to set out the expected benefits of building the line.

By the projected railroad, the movement of goods between Liverpool and Manchester will be accomplished in four or five hours and the charges to the merchant will be reduced by at least one third. The immediate advantages of the proposed line are improved methods for the general operation of commerce and financial savings to the trading community. The inhabitants of these busy towns will receive their full share of direct benefits. Coal will be brought to market in greater quantity and at reduced price. Farming produce of various kinds will find its way from greater distances at cheaper rates. To landowners, also, near the line, the railway offers important advantages in extensive markets for their agricultural produce, as well as a means of obtaining lime and manure at a low rate in return. As a cheap and fast way to travel for passengers, the railroad holds out a fair prospect to the public.

Source C: a nineteenth-century cartoon from *Punch* magazine which reflects some contemporary opinions. An opponent of the railways, dressed as a medieval knight, but poorly armed, tries to halt the wheels of progress.

Question

Using **ALL** the sources and your own knowledge, were the railways welcomed by all?

24 The Great Reform Bill, 1832

Read the introduction and the sources and then answer the question which follows.

→ Introduction

In June 1832, the Reform Bill became law, but only after a long struggle to steer it through Parliament. In the end, Wellington and many Tory opponents of the Bill stayed away from the Lords so that Grey could achieve his political success. Many who supported the Bill feared a social revolution unless they acted. Radical leaders like William Cobbett and Henry Hunt demanded a widening of the right to vote. Organisations such as the National Union of the Working Class also wanted political change. However, in 1832 members of the working class were to be disappointed.

Source A: an extract from a modern writer describing some of the political and social effects of the Bill.

But what did the Bill do? There was never any question of allowing all men to vote, as the upper class would have been swamped. In boroughs, the vote was given to householders worth more than £10 per year. In the countryside it went to 40/- [£2] freeholders. Owing to these changes, about one sixth of the male population had the vote. Although industrial interests were more represented, landowners remained strong. For example in the Parliament of 1841–1846, over 70% of MPs came from the landed classes. The Bill did not introduce a secret ballot and the working class was still excluded from the franchise. The political reforms of 1832 favoured the middle classes and the Bill was not as far reaching as some reformers had hoped.

Source B: part of a speech in Parliament by Thomas Babington Macaulay in March 1831. Macaulay was a young man who supported the cause of reform.

Unhappily, the lower orders in England are occasionally in a state of great distress, poverty and suffering. We know what effect distress produces. We know that it makes even wise men irritable and unreasonable. When eager for immediate relief, distress blunts their judgement, and it inflames their passions. I support this measure because I am sure it is our best security against a revolution. I support this measure as a measure of reform, but I support it still more as a way of preserving ourselves [the middle and upper classes].

Source C: a nineteenth-century engraving showing Queen Square, Bristol, during Reform Bill riots on the night of 30 October 1831. Other riots in London and Derby frightened the upper classes, hinting at possible revolution from below and prompting some MPs to support reform from above, before it was too late.

Question

Using **ALL** the sources and your own knowledge, did the Reform Bill really bring much change?

The Chartists

Read the introduction and the sources and then answer the question which follows.

→ Introduction

The Chartists were a group of working-class political reformers seeking the vote for all men. They were so named because they presented their ideas in the form of a six-point Charter. This Charter, along with petitions requesting various social and economic improvements, was submitted to Parliament in 1839, 1842 and 1848. Although it was rejected at each presentation, some of the Chartist ideals lived on through the work of other reforming movements.

Source A: an extract from a modern writer discussing the extent of the Chartists' achievements.

In the short term, the Chartists failed. Their petitions were heavily rejected by a House of Commons dominated by the landed class. Riots, such as those at Newport in 1839, were crushed and served mainly to increase government suspicion of the movement. Economic recovery during the 1840s weakened Chartism, and Chartist opposition to the Anti-Corn Law League cut them off from a successful reforming group whose aims also favoured the working class. On the other hand, Chartism made some of the upper classes reconsider their views, and sympathy for reform grew. Political rights for the working class, although largely achieved through the Reform Bills of 1867 and 1884, owed something to the influence of Chartism. Chartist ideals of a secret ballot and payment of MPs were achieved in 1872 and 1911 respectively. Of the Charter's six points, five are now practised.

Source B: from a speech by Thomas Attwood introducing the Charter and the First Petition to Parliament on 14 June 1839. Attwood was a great supporter of the Chartists.

[Thomas Attwood said] the Petition originated in the town of Birmingham. It was forwarded to Glasgow where it received the signatures of 90,000 honest men. I hold in my hand a list of two hundred and fourteen towns and villages in different parts of Great Britain where the Petition has been adopted and signed and it is now presented with 1,280,000 signatures. The men who signed the Petition were honest and industrious, men of sober and unblemished character, men who have discharged the duties of good members of society and who have always obeyed the laws.

Source C: a nineteenth-century engraving showing Thomas Duncombe presenting the Second Petition to Parliament in May 1842. This Petition contained more than three million signatures. Despite short-term failures, the Chartists may still be seen as an effective pressure group.

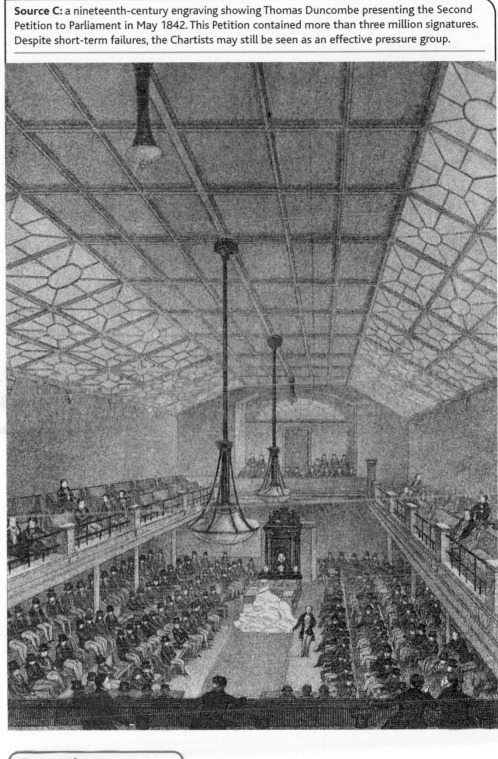

Question

Using **ALL** the sources and your own knowledge, how far do you consider Chartism a failure?

26 The Crimean War, 1854–56

Read the introduction and the sources and then answer the question which follows.

→ ## Introduction

Keen to prevent any Tsarist expansion into Europe at Turkish expense, which could threaten her political and economic power, Britain fought against the Russians in the Crimean War. Despite allied victories at the battles of the Alma, Balaclava and Inkerman, the war proved costly with more than 45,000 British and 180,000 French casualties. Much of this huge death toll resulted from disease, lack of supplies and military mismanagement. The Treaty of Paris did not resolve the Eastern Question and within eight years, Europe was nearly at war again over Russian claims in the Near East.

Source A: an extract from a modern writer discussing the effects of the Treaty of Paris signed at the end of the Crimean War.

The final treaty was signed at Paris on 30 March 1856. By the treaty, the Straits Convention of 1841 was re-stated and the Dardanelles closed to warships of all foreign nations in times of peace. In addition, the Russians were banned from building naval or military fortifications on the shores of the Black Sea. Russia was also to abandon her claim to be the protector of the Orthodox Christians in the Turkish Empire. Russian influence in the Balkans was reduced and her naval power was now no longer a threat to the power of Britain and France in the Mediterranean. However, none of these agreements lasted long and in 1870, during the Franco-Prussian War, Russia declared that she was no longer bound by the terms of the Treaty of Paris.

Source B: from a report on the Battle of Inkerman written for the *New York Times* on 5 November 1854. Described as a 'soldier's battle', the conflict consisted of a series of disconnected encounters by individual units with many examples of personal heroism. The Russians lost 12,000 troops. Allied killed or wounded amounted to 3,500 men.

And now commenced the bloodiest struggle ever witnessed since war cursed the earth. It has been doubted by military historians if any enemy has ever stood firm against a charge with the bayonet. It was believed that no foe could withstand the British soldier wielding his favourite weapon. Here, the bayonet was often the only weapon employed in fights of the most deadly character. There were desperate encounters between men, carried out with the bayonet alone. The British and French resisted, bayonet to bayonet, the Russian infantry, as they charged again and again with incredible fury and determination. The battle became a series of dreadful deeds of daring and of bloody hand-to-hand fights. Finally, the battalions of the Tsar gave way and the Russians sullenly retired.

Source C: an illustration of the Light Brigade charging into the Valley of Death on 25 October 1854 at the Battle of Balaclava. The charge provides a perfect example of heroism, military blundering and blindly obedient courage.

Question

Using **ALL** the sources and your own knowledge, how successful was the Crimean War?

27 The Indian Mutiny, 1857

Read the introduction and the sources and then answer the question which follows.

→ Introduction

On 10 May 1857, Indian troops in the British Army [Sepoys] shot their officers and mutinied. Other Sepoy regiments of the North-West provinces followed suit. The English settlements at Cawnpore and Lucknow were besieged and the European inhabitants were massacred. There was horror and brutality on both sides and for a time it seemed as though the whole of British power in India would crumble. However, the Mutiny never turned into a full war of independence. The revolt scarcely affected one-third of British India and order was restored quickly. Nonetheless, some changes were later made to the way India was governed.

Source A: an extract from a British account dated 1857, of the Cawnpore Massacre by the men of Nana Sahib. After recapture by the British, the rebels were made to lick two square inches of floor clean of blood, before being hanged.

The women and children were dispatched [killed] first with swords and spears. The men were arranged in line, with a bamboo running along the whole extent and passing through each man's arms, which were tied at the back. The troops then rode about them and taunted their victims. One of them would fire a pistol in the face of a captive, whose shattered head would drop to the right or left. Not a single soul escaped.

Source B: a modern writer commenting on changes to the government of India following the Mutiny. These new arrangements failed to prevent many Indians from striving for further political reform.

In August 1858, the India Act transferred the government of India from the East India Company to the British Crown. By this, the Governor-General of the Company became a Viceroy. The new Indian Civil Service inherited many of the former administrators of the Company and its forces became part of the new Indian Army. Sadly, however, the Mutiny had left a legacy of bitterness which was never completely healed, in view of the atrocities committed by both sides. Although for the next decades, about 5,000 British and Indian civil servants, backed by a small army, were found capable of ruling the country, leading Indians naturally dreamed of a united, independent land of their own.

Source C: an illustration from *The History of the Indian Mutiny*, a book published in 1858, showing rebel Sepoys being blown to bits from the mouth of British guns.

Question

Using **ALL** the sources and your own knowledge, how far do you agree that the Indian Mutiny doomed British control of India?

Slavery

Read the introduction and the sources and then answer the question which follows.

→ ## Introduction

Throughout the eighteenth and early nineteenth centuries, thousands of black Africans from West Africa were taken in British ships to work as slaves in the Americas. This was part of the so-called Triangular Trade. British ships took goods to Africa, then carried African slaves to the sugar plantations, finally sailing back home with goods produced by slave labour. Economic gain and profit mattered more than any social pain and misery involved. The slave trade was eventually abolished in 1807, although it was not until 1833 that slavery was formally ended within the British Empire.

Source A: an extract from a modern historian discussing the position of the slave trade. Slavery was regarded as essential to the exploitation of the West Indian colonies. These were seen as the keystone of British imperial prosperity. Human welfare was largely disregarded until the anti-slavery campaigns began.

Britain's share of the slave trade became the largest of all European countries. Between 1701 and 1800 about 2.5 million of the 6.13 million slaves exported were taken for British business interests. This reflected the expanding demand for labour from British plantations, especially the sugar colonies. The trade was viewed as a pillar of the plantations and necessary to commercial and economic expansion. The slave trade was conducted both through private companies as well as trading individuals. Slaves were exchanged for an increasing number of English products, as varied as Devon textiles and iron manufactures from Birmingham. Most classes of British society were directly or indirectly involved in the slave trade. Lawyers, parliamentarians and churchmen viewed it as justifiable.

Source B: a nineteenth-century eyewitness describes scenes on a slave ship. Conditions were wretched. Slaves lacked adequate food, water or room. The stench was appalling and the whole atmosphere inhuman.

The ship had taken in 336 males and 226 females on the coast of Africa, making in all 562, and had been out at sea seventeen days, during which she had thrown overboard 55. The slaves were all enclosed under grated hatchways between decks. The space was so low that they sat between each other's legs and were stowed [packed in] so close together that there was no possibility of their lying down or at all changing their positions night or day. The greater part were shut out from light or air. They were branded like sheep with the owner's marks in different forms, burnt onto their bodies with a red-hot iron. Some were greatly emaciated [very thin], and some, particularly children, seemed dying.

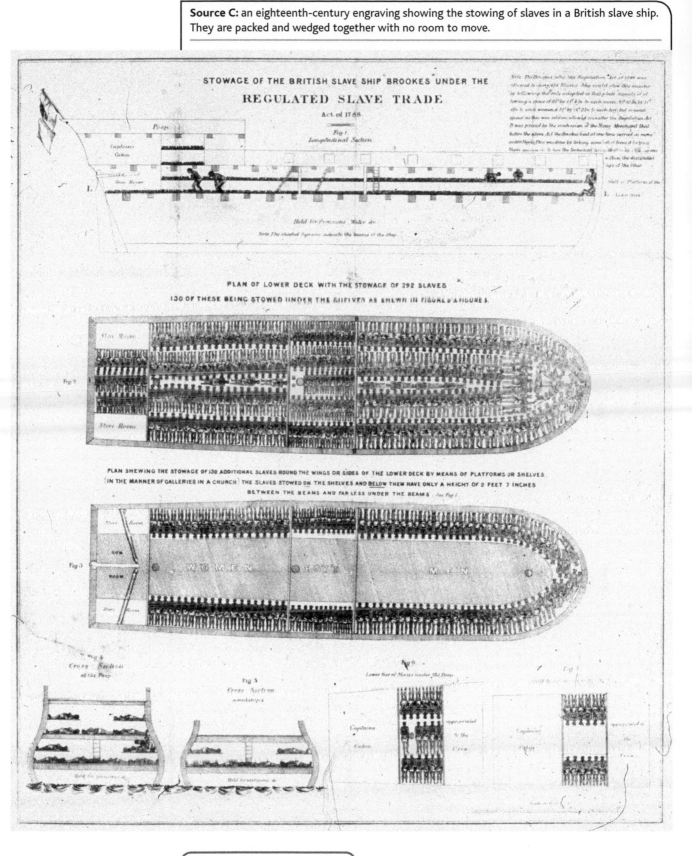

Source C: an eighteenth-century engraving showing the stowing of slaves in a British slave ship. They are packed and wedged together with no room to move.

Question

Using **ALL** the sources and your own knowledge, how far do you agree that the slave trade benefited Britain?

Public health

Read the introduction and the sources and then answer the question which follows.

→ ## Introduction

During the latter part of the nineteenth century, a series of government laws was introduced in a bid to improve public health. More hospitals were built and local areas became responsible for the provision of improved water supplies and sanitation. Individuals such as Edwin Chadwick, whose passion for the public good led to major improvements in the life of many, also played their part. A third factor was the fear of diseases like cholera, which reappeared frequently.

Source A: an extract from a modern historian commenting on some of the factors which encouraged the government to take steps to improve public health.

In 1842, Chadwick made his Report on The Sanitary Conditions of the Labouring Population, and in 1844, another on The Health of the Towns. These reports led to the first Public Health Act in 1848, which permitted local boards of health to be set up to improve sanitation, water supply and drainage. The Public Health Act, 1875, made important new demands upon the local authorities. They had to appoint Medical Officers of Health, improve water supplies, ensure adequate drainage and sewage disposal and collect refuse regularly. Inspectors of nuisances were appointed and the authorities had to see that any polluted food was destroyed.

Source B: an extract from Edwin Chadwick's Report after an Inquiry into *The Sanitary Conditions of the Labouring Population of Great Britain*, London, 1842. This Report greatly influenced the government of Lord John Russell and led to the first Public Health Act in 1848.

The various forms of epidemics, and other diseases, chiefly amongst the labouring classes, result from atmospheric impurities [nasty smells] produced by decomposing animal and vegetable substances, by damp and filth, and by close and overcrowded houses. Where those circumstances are removed by drainage, proper cleansing and better ventilation, the frequency and intensity of such disease is lessened. Where the removal of the noxious agencies [harmful things] appears to be complete, such disease almost entirely disappears. The primary and most important measures, and at the same time the most practicable, are good drainage, the removal of all refuse from streets and roads, and the improvement of the supplies of water.

Source C: a nineteenth-century illustration of the Fleet Street Sewer. In 1859, after a law designed to reduce water pollution in the Thames, work began to build a proper sewage system for London. A 1,300-mile network of brick tunnels was constructed. It was complete by 1875 and extended in 1879. Further improvements followed in the years after 1900. Cholera became much less common by the end of the century, suggesting that efforts by local authorities to improve public health had enjoyed some success.

Question

Using **ALL** the sources and your own knowledge, how far is it true that major improvements to public health in the 1800s were achieved mainly through the work of individuals rather than official authorities?

30 The Suffragettes

Read the introduction and the sources and then answer the question which follows.

→ ## Introduction

The Suffragettes were a militant group who demanded the vote for women. This was partly granted in 1918 and fully achieved ten years later. Suffragettes used aggressive methods such as chaining themselves to railings, setting fire to letterboxes, smashing shop windows, destroying turf on golf courses and, in one case, 'martyrdom' under the King's horse at the Epsom Derby of 1913. Such tactics antagonised many women and frightened the very authorities who had the power to grant reform. It was said that the extremists weakened the cause they championed. On the other hand, the vital contribution of women to the First World War undoubtedly helped them win greater political influence.

Source A: an extract from a modern historian commenting on the activities of militant suffragettes and on other factors which won limited voting rights for women in 1918.

Women had begun to demand the right to vote (i.e. the suffrage) in the 19th century, but in Edward VII's reign their appeals became much more insistent. The more militant 'suffragettes' were prepared to go to almost any lengths in order to achieve their aims (e.g. by tying themselves to railings, attacking policemen or slashing pictures at the National Gallery). When suffragettes were imprisoned for breaking the law, they refused to eat. During the 1914–1918 War the Suffragette campaign was halted while women proved by their service as nurses, drivers and munitions factory workers that they were worthy to vote and as a result in 1918 the first voting rights were granted to females over thirty.

Source B: part of an article from *The Morning Post* of 8 May 1913. The headlines read, 'BOMB AT ST. PAUL'S – UNSUCCESSFUL ATTEMPT TO WRECK CHANCEL – SUPPOSED SUFFRAGETTE OUTRAGE'. Such attacks on churches disgusted many people, leading to a feeling that perhaps women did not deserve the vote.

An explosive device [bomb] was found near the Bishop's Throne in the chancel of St. Paul's Cathedral yesterday morning a few minutes prior to the celebration of early Communion. There is no doubt in the minds of the authorities that it was designed and placed there by someone associated with the militant Suffragist movement. The bomb was carefully wrapped in brown paper and in part of a recent issue of the militant newspaper The Suffragette. An expert stated that while such a bomb as that found at St. Paul's would have done relatively little damage to that building because of the great air spaces which exist within it, a similar device in Westminster Abbey might result in permanent damage to the historic structure.

Source C: an image from *The Illustrated London News* in 1912. The picture shows Suffragettes smashing shop windows. Such disregard of public order led many people, women as well as men, to feel only contempt for their cause.

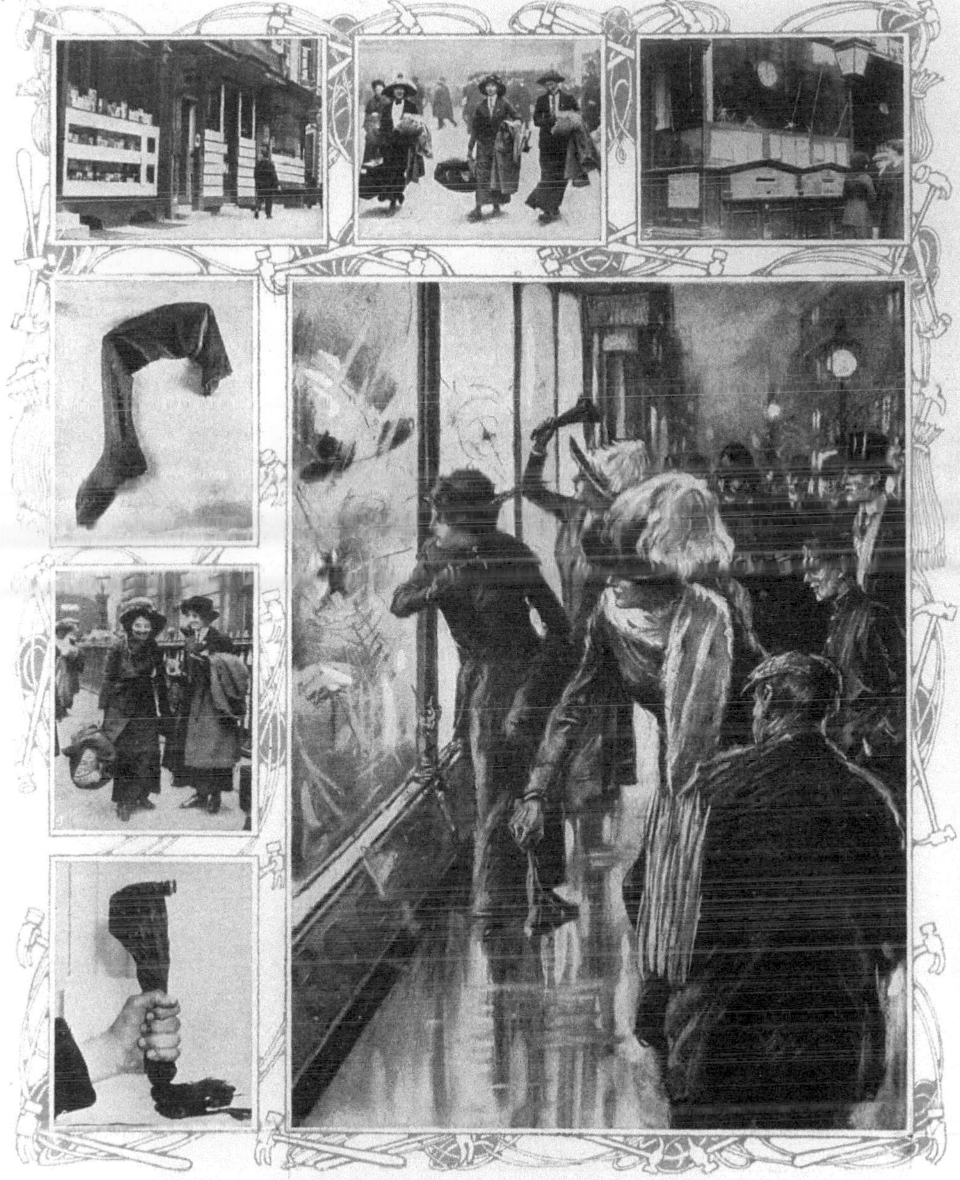

THE ILLUSTRATED LONDON NEWS, MARCH 9, 1912.–353

GLASS - SMASHING FOR VOTES! SUFFRAGETTES AS WINDOW - BREAKERS.

DRAWING BY WILMOT LUNT; PHOTOGRAPHS BY L.N.A., SPORT AND GENERAL, AND TOPICAL.

1. TACTICS THE POLICE ADVISED SHOPKEEPERS TO FOLLOW FOR MONDAY NIGHT, MARCH 4: WINDOWS BROKEN BY SUFFRAGETTES ON MARCH 1 BARRICADED.
2. ACCUSED OF WINDOW-SMASHING AND READY FOR PRISON: SUFFRAGETTES ARRIVING FOR TRIAL AT BOW STREET, WITH THEIR LUGGAGE.
3. ILLUSTRATING THE DAMAGE DONE AND SHOWING THE FORM TAKEN BY THE MAJORITY OF THE "BREAKS": THE SMASHED WINDOWS OF REGENT STREET POST OFFICE.

[illegible] USED TO BREAK THE WINDOWS: A STOCKING CONTAINING A HAMMER, FOUND IN THE MIDDLE OF THE ROAD IN REGENT STREET.

5. A SUFFRAGETTE LEADER WITH THE BUNDLE OF A FRIEND DETERMINED TO GO TO PRISON: MRS. PETHICK LAWRENCE ARRIVING AT BOW STREET TO BE PRESENT AT THE TRIAL.
6. PICKED UP INSIDE A BROKEN WINDOW IN THE HAYMARKET: A DOROTHY BAG CONTAINING A HAMMER.
7. THE DEMONSTRATION AS SEEN BY ONE OF OUR ARTISTS, WHO CHANCED TO BE ON THE SPOT AT THE MOMENT: SUFFRAGETTES BREAKING WINDOWS IN OXFORD STREET.

The militant Suffragettes made another most remarkable attempt to draw public attention to their cause the other day by indulging in a window-smashing campaign which began just before six o'clock in the evening on Friday, March 1. Shop-front after shop-front in the West-End, and in the West Central district as far as Chancery Lane, was smashed by women, who carried hammers in Dorothy bags or concealed in some other manner. After they had done damage estimated at between £4000 and £5000, most of the women were captured, and a number of them were brought before the Magistrate at Bow Street on the Saturday and were sentenced. In all, 124 surrendered to their bail. The Suffragettes announced a further "surprise" for the Monday; whereupon the police warned shopkeepers and others to close their shutters and barricade their windows. On the Monday morning they began window-breaking again; and, for instance, attacked glass at Messrs. Harrod's, at shops in Kensington and Knightsbridge, at the Lord Chancellor's, and at Lord Crewe's.

Question

Using **ALL** the sources and your own knowledge, do you think it is true to say that the militant tactics of the Suffragettes did more harm than good to their cause?

SAMPLE ESSAY QUESTIONS
1066–1914

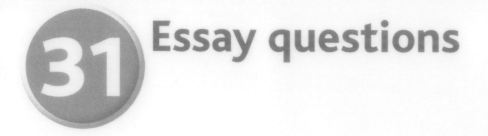

Essay questions

These titles cover all three Common Entrance time periods from 1066 to 1914. They are grouped around the five study themes: war and rebellion; government and parliament; religion; social and economic history, and general topics, including local history, which are common to all historical periods.

→ War and rebellion

1 Choose a war which you have studied and explain its most important causes.

2 Explain the consequences of any one war which you have studied.

3 Explain the significance of any battle you have studied.

4 Choose any military commander and explain why he or she was successful.

5 Explain the causes of any one rebellion you have studied.

6 Choose any rebellion you have studied and explain the extent to which it threatened the government of the day.

7 Assess the reasons for the failure of any rebellion in the period you have studied.

8 Choose any rebellion you have studied and explain the role of the rebel leader.

→ Government and parliament

9 Explain the importance of the work of any one government minister.

10 Choose a chief minister you have studied and explain the reasons for his fall from power.

11 Choose any important event in the history of Parliament and explain why it should be remembered.

12 Choose one monarch who clashed with Parliament and assess his or her success or failure.

13 Describe a political movement you have studied and explain its significance.

14 Choose a political thinker from the period you have studied and explain how important his or her ideas were.

→ Religion

15 Explain why religion has been so important in any one period you have studied.

16 Choose any one religious leader and explain the importance of his or her ideas.

17 Explain how the Church helped in the lives of people in any period you have studied.

18 Explain how religious arguments helped to shape the beliefs of the Church in any period you have studied.

→ Social and economic history

19 Explain the significance of the changes to daily life in any period you have studied.

20 Choose a major historical event which altered the lives of people and explain its significance.

21 Explain how the poor were cared for in any period you have studied.

22 Explain the role of women in any period of history you have studied.

23 Explain the importance of the development of Britain's overseas territories in any period you have studied.

24 Choose any important building in England/Britain and explain its significance for the lives of people.

25 Describe a piece of art or music from the period you have studied, and explain its significance.

26 Assess the importance for England/Britain of any one technological development.

→ General topics

27 Choose a local historical site that you know well. Explain its importance to that particular area of the country and to history in general.

28 Explain the significance of any one item which you have seen on a visit to a museum.

29 Choose any artist or writer who you think has made the greatest contribution to England/Britain and explain why his or her achievement is so important.

30 Explain the importance of any one invention which changed the lives of people in any period you have studied.